POSTCARD HISTORY SERIES

Texas Oil
and Gas

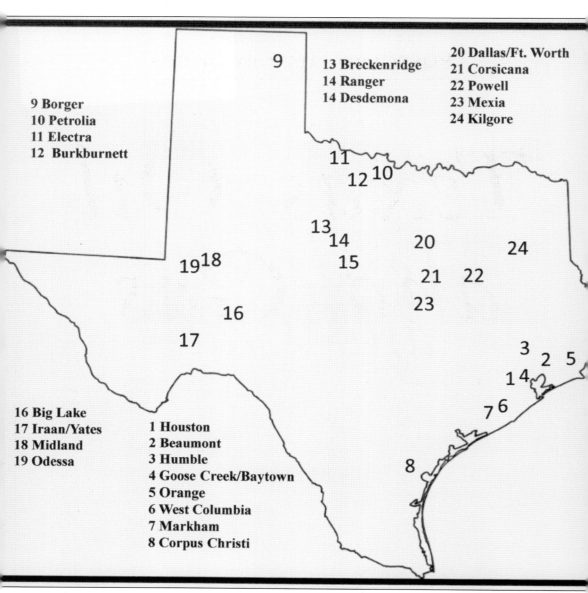

9 Borger
10 Petrolia
11 Electra
12 Burkburnett

13 Breckenridge
14 Ranger
14 Desdemona

20 Dallas/Ft. Worth
21 Corsicana
22 Powell
23 Mexia
24 Kilgore

16 Big Lake
17 Iraan/Yates
18 Midland
19 Odessa

1 Houston
2 Beaumont
3 Humble
4 Goose Creek/Baytown
5 Orange
6 West Columbia
7 Markham
8 Corpus Christi

Oil and gas production occurs throughout much of Texas. This reference map locates many of the oil fields and cities discussed in Texas Oil and Gas.

ON THE COVER: More than a dozen wooden oil derricks dot the Spindletop landscape south of Beaumont. In less than a year after the oil field's Lucas Gusher discovery well, 300 derricks would cover the area.

POSTCARD HISTORY SERIES

Texas Oil and Gas

Jeff A. Spencer

ARCADIA
PUBLISHING

Copyright © 2013 by Jeff A. Spencer
ISBN 978-1-4671-3021-9

Published by Arcadia Publishing
Charleston, South Carolina

Printed in the United States of America

Library of Congress Control Number: 2013906230

For all general information contact Arcadia Publishing at:
Telephone 843-853-2070
Fax 843-853-0044
E-mail sales@arcadiapublishing.com
For customer service and orders:
Toll-Free 1-888-313-2665

Visit us on the Internet at www.arcadiapublishing.com

*To Texas oil and gas explorers, oil field workers, and oil producers,
past and present.*

CONTENTS

ACKNOWLEDGMENTS

Historians are finding it more costly to use postcard and photographic collections of many museums and university libraries. Per-image usage fees of $40 to $50 add up quickly, especially for books that include more than 100 images. For that reason, it is refreshing when an author has an opportunity to work with individuals and institutions that provide the use of historical images at little to no cost.

Much thanks goes to D. Ryan Smith, executive director of the Texas Energy Museum of Beaumont. Ryan accommodated my two visits to this excellent museum's archives, allowing me to scan several postcards. I greatly enjoyed our conversations on the history of the Spindletop area. Grace Charles, librarian information specialist, Special Collections & Archives, Bell Library at Texas A&M University—Corpus Christi, saved me a four-hour drive by scanning a few postcards from the Dan Gilmore Papers Collection and e-mailing them to me. In Bay City, Texas, the Matagorda County Museum's archives contain many photographs of the area's early oil history. Jennifer Rodgers, archives and collections manager, was kind enough to search out a few excellent oil field postcards within the museum's extensive photograph collection. Carol Gibbs of the Matagorda County Historical Commission also shared her knowledge of the county's oil field history. The staff of the Humble Museum, in Humble, Texas, welcomed my wife and I during our visit, showed us the museum's oil field artifacts and photographs, and allowed me to scan postcards from the museum's collection. Thanks also to Nancy Coker, president of the board of directors of the Humble Museum.

Fellow postcard collectors and historians are always a cooperative source of material. Thanks go to Victoria Manning of Brooklyn, New York, for our discussions on a classic early oil tank fire image. Her web page contains a fascinating compilation, both historic and artistic, of this interesting and well-traveled image. Edward Lynn Williams of Farmers Branch, Texas, welcomed me to the Dallas area and allowed me to scan many of his oil-related postcards of Navarro County. Susan Davidek Svec of Boling, Texas, had graciously allowed me to scan postcards from her collection for two previous oil history projects, and I thank her for providing material for this book.

Lastly, to my wife, Linda, and daughters, Emily and Rebecca, thank you for your patience as I researched and compiled the material for *Texas Oil and Gas*.

Unless otherwise noted in the captions, all images appear courtesy of the author.

INTRODUCTION

In the early 20th century, picture postcards were both a means of communication and popular collectibles. The 1901 Spindletop oil discovery near Beaumont, Texas, occurred just a few years before the golden age of postcard collecting (1907–1915), and early photographs of this field became postcards. In 1903, Eastman Kodak developed a folding pocket camera, allowing the general public to take photographs and print them directly onto paper with postcard backs. These postcards became known as real-photo postcards (RPPCs), and many excellent oil field images were captured in this format. Texas pioneer photographers, including Frank Trost (1868–1944), Frank J. Schlueter (1874–1972), Benjamin Harrison Loden (1875–1926), and Jack Nolan (1889–1972), captured the hustle and bustle of the oil boomtowns as well as spectacular images of oil gushers and oil field fires. Many of their photographs became postcards.

Though many associate the 1901 Lucas oil gusher at Spindletop with the beginning of the state's petroleum industry, the use of oil in Texas occurred hundreds of years earlier. Native Americans and early Spanish explorers collected oil from natural oil seeps. In 1543, members of Hernando de Soto's expedition used oil collected along the Texas Gulf Coast to caulk their boats. In 1866, near Oil Springs, Lyne T. Barret drilled Texas's first well-producing oil. The state's first significant oil field, Corsicana, was discovered in 1894 during drilling for a water well.

The generally accepted source of the name Spindletop is a grove of trees on a mound shaped like an inverted spindle top. Associated with this mound were gas seeps and sour water wells. Patillo Higgins, a "self-taught geologist," was convinced that there was oil beneath this mound, despite the conclusions of experts from Standard Oil and the US Geological Survey. In 1893, W.B. Sharpe and J.S. Cullinan drilled a well to 418 feet, encountering only minor amounts of gas at a depth of 60 feet. Higgins drilled and completed a well to this gas sand to supply fuel for his oil rig's boiler.

In 1899, Capt. Anthony F. Lucas, a mining engineer, arrived in Beaumont. With financial backing from Pittsburgh oilmen James Guffey and John Galey, Lucas drilled a well to 575 feet, recovering minor amounts of oil. In October 1900, Lucas began another well on the southwest side of the mound. On January 10, 1901, while drilling at a depth of 1,139 feet, the well "blew in," spewing a six-inch stream of oil 150–200 feet into the air. The "Lucas Gusher" had an estimated flow of 70,000–90,000 barrels of oil per day. At the time of the Spindletop discovery, the entire state of Texas was producing less than 2,400 barrels of oil per day.

People flocked to see the Spindletop oil gushers. The Southern Pacific Railroad ran excursion trains from Beaumont. Newspaper articles compared Spindletop to the Russian oil fields at Baku. The population of Beaumont quickly soared from approximately 10,000 to more than 50,000.

The discovery of oil at Spindletop affected the future growth and development of Texas and the nation. Soon, railroads and steamships converted from coal to the abundant and cheap oil for fuel. The construction of refineries, pipelines, and shipping facilities followed.

The search for additional oil fields spread throughout the Texas and Louisiana Gulf Coast. Northwest of Beaumont, in Hardin County, areas with surface indications similar to Spindletop suggested the presence of underlying oil. As early as 1859, oil seeps were recognized near the town of Saratoga, and wells drilled in 1865 and 1896 encountered minor flows of oil and gas. Native Americans recognized the health benefits of mineral springs near present-day Sour Springs many years before the Sour Lake Springs health resort was built in the 1850s. During the first decade of the 1900s, substantial oil fields were discovered at Sour Lake (1902), Saratoga (1902), Batson (1903), Humble (1905), and Goose Creek (1908).

Oil operators and wildcatters then looked beyond the oil discoveries of the Gulf Coast. In North Texas, near the town of Petrolia, gas seeps had been known since the early 1900s. With the completion of the first gas well near the town in 1907, North Texas counties attracted additional drilling. In 1911, oil was discovered near the town of Electra, and the North Texas oil boom began, culminating with the oil gushers of Burkburnett in 1918. Nearby Wichita Falls saw a rapid increase in population. In just over two years, the population grew from approximately 8,000 to more than 40,000.

On the recommendation of geologist Charles Gould, the Amarillo Oil Company leased 64,000 acres north of Amarillo. The company's first well, completed on December 9, 1918, flowed between 10 and 15 million cubic feet of gas per day. With continued drilling, the dimensions of the Panhandle gas field proved staggering! The field, encompassing parts of eight counties, had a length of more than 115 miles and a width of over 20 miles. Oil was discovered in the area in 1921, but the area's true oil boom began near Borger in 1926.

In North Central Texas, oil discoveries were made at Ranger (1917), Desdemona (1918), and Breckenridge (1918). "The Boom that Won the War" was attributed to the timing of the Ranger oil boom, providing much-needed oil for the Allied forces in Europe. The 1920s opened with the discovery of the Mexia oil field in Central Texas. Unlike the Gulf Coast salt dome oil fields or the large geologic structures of the North Texas and Panhandle oil fields, the productive sands at Mexia were trapped along a fault. This revelation opened up additional areas of exploration in Texas, and other "fault-line" oil fields were discovered within the next four years at Curie, Powell, Richland, and Wortham.

The Permian Basin of West Texas and Southeastern New Mexico covers an area approximately 250 miles wide by 300 miles long, including portions of 52 counties. Before 1921, West Texas was known as the "petroleum graveyard of Texas." While drilling water wells, ranchers had occasionally found traces of oil as early as 1901, but it was 20 years before the first oil well was completed. Mitchell County's Westbrook oil field, discovered in 1921, was the first commercial oil field in the area. Big Lake oil field confirmed the great oil potential of West Texas. Midland grew as the financial center of the Permian Basin, while Odessa became the industrial and petrochemical hub. Approximately 30 billion barrels of oil and 75 trillion cubic feet of gas have been produced from the Permian Basin. Within the basin, four fields have produced over one billion barrels of oil each.

The giant East Texas oil field was discovered in 1930 with "Dad" Joiner's No. 3 Daisy Bradford well. With continued drilling, the field's dimensions were established as 42 miles long with an average width of 4.5 miles, including portions of five counties. The field, the largest oil field in the contiguous United States, has produced more than five billion barrels of oil.

The history of the petroleum industry in Texas covers a large part of the state and is still being written. Advances in technology have revived many old producing areas. In 2011, Texas led the nation in oil production, with more than 390 million barrels of oil.

One

SPINDLETOP AND THE GOLDEN TRIANGLE

This famous view of the Lucas gusher was captured by Port Arthur photographer Frank J. Trost on the afternoon of January 10, 1901. The postcard's caption reads, "Lucas Gusher—Gushing 270 feet. 70,000 BBLS [barrels] Daily." Trost's photograph appeared in newspapers all across the United States and in some foreign newspapers. In just a few months, Trost sold 45,000 copies of the photograph at 50¢ each.

There were 6 oil gushers on "The Hill" by April 1901; 65 by October. Workers flocked to Beaumont, and the city's population increased from 9,000 to more than 50,000 during 1901, stabilizing somewhat around 20,000 the next year. Within the first year, over 500 oil and land companies operated out of Beaumont. Hotels were full, so men slept in the lobbies or rented rooms from local residents.

By 1902, the average cost of a Spindletop well was $7,429. Potential investors rushed to the area. "Side-gushers" or "sidesaddle gushers" were wells whose oil flow was reopened, often days after the well had been capped, to impress investors or for the enjoyment of sightseers. A close look at this scene shows men dressed in suits on the derrick floor.

GUSHER BURNING, BEAUMONT, TEX.

A discarded cigar was responsible for one of the first oil-well fires at Spindletop, on September 12, 1902. The well was operated by the Texas Flora Oil Company. The fire spread to 20 wells, several oil storage tanks, and an oil-pumping station.

The "Philp Bros." began operations at Spindletop in 1902. Joseph, Will, and John were pioneer oil operators in the field, and the Philp Brothers Oil Company operated out of Beaumont for at least 50 years. In 1903, "Brother" Will Philp helped organize a Methodist Sunday school and church near Spindletop, serving as a minister.

"Boiler Avenue" was the site of some of the densest drilling at Spindletop. It was said that a person could walk from one oil derrick to the next without stepping on the ground. The original photograph, dated April 23, 1903, was taken by H.L. Edgerton, who had opened a studio in the nearby boomtown of Gladys City. A reproduction of Edgerton's studio can be visited at the Spindletop Gladys City Boomtown Museum.

The caption of this postcard reads, "On the line of the Southern Pacific R.R." The Southern Pacific Railroad advertised its line through Texas and Louisiana's rice, sugar, and oil fields. With the oil gushers of Spindletop and Jennings, in Louisiana, in 1901, the company recognized the potential of oil as fuel and announced that it would be converting from coal-burning to oil-fired engines.

Many of the early Spindletop wells flowed at high oil rates, like this 75,000-barrel-per-day well, gushing "225 feet high." The Heywood Brothers drilled one of the more notable gushers in the field. Their No. 2 well, which flowed an estimated 96,000 barrels of oil per day, at the time was touted as the greatest gusher in the world.

Oil Gusher, BEAUMONT, Tex. 75,000 Bbl. Daily Gushing 225 feet high.

The J.M. Guffey Petroleum Company was granted a Texas charter on May 16, 1901, and opened an office in Beaumont. The company constructed a pumping station and storage facilities near Beaumont and completed a pipeline to Port Arthur, where oil was pumped to the company's small refinery. Port Arthur is 17 miles southeast of Beaumont on Sabine Lake, with access to the Gulf of Mexico.

Guffey Oil Station, Beaumont, Tex.

Guffey signed a two-year contract with the Timmons brothers of Cleveland, Ohio, to design the refinery stills for the production of kerosene from Spindletop oil. A 100-barrel-a-day and a 375-barrel-a-day still were built in Ohio and shipped to Texas. This first attempt to refine the heavier Texas crude oil was not entirely successful.

The Mellons of Pittsburgh financed the J.M. Guffey Company. In 1907, the Mellons combined the Guffey Company with Gulf Refining Company and Gulf Pipeline Company, creating the Gulf Oil Corporation. The Port Arthur refinery was renamed and expanded. By 1916, it was one of the three largest refineries in the nation.

A Portion of the Fleet of
The Gulf Refining Company, Port Arthur, Texas,
loading oil for Northern Markets.

J.M. Guffey Petroleum Company built a five-tanker fleet to transport oil to Northern markets. The first steamer, the *Atlas*, left Sabine Pass on March 11, 1901, with 3,000 barrels of oil. Guffey's fleet became part of the Gulf Oil Corporation in 1907.

Aerial View, Gulf Oil Corporation Refineries, Port Arthur, Texas

In 1915, Gulf's Port Arthur refinery began experiments that led to the manufacturing of aluminum chloride, used to produce gasoline. During the 1920s, Gulf built 27 stills, each with a 1,000-barrel-a-day capacity, to produce gasoline. By 1923, the expanded Port Arthur refinery was the largest in the world. Gulf Oil was acquired by Chevron in 1984. Clark Refining purchased the refinery in 1995 and changed the name to Premcor in 2000. Valero purchased the refinery in 2005.

Burt Refinery, Beaumont, Tex.

In December 1901, George Burt purchased 89 acres for a refinery site. Located three miles south of Spindletop, along the Neches River, the land cost $45,000. The George A. Burt and Company refinery opened on May 1, 1903. It was widely suspected that Burt had ties with Standard Oil. The Security Oil Company took over all of Burt's assets 12 days later.

OIL STEAMERS WAITING TO BE LOADED AT MAGNOLIA PETROLEUM CO. DOCKS, BEAUMONT, TEXAS.

Just two months after the Spindletop discovery, crude oil was being transported to refineries along the East Coast. The Neches River provided an outlet to the Gulf of Mexico by way of Sabine Pass. Magnolia constructed a 1,000-foot reinforced concrete wharf and dock facilities.

By early 1902, there were nine refineries in the planning stage or under construction in the Beaumont–Port Arthur area. Among the firms building refineries were George A. Burt and Company, Union Oil & Refining, Central-Asphalt & Refining, W.E. Brice, and the Texas Company. Guffey had already completed its refinery.

The John Sealy Company purchased the Security (Burt) refinery in 1909. In 1911, the refinery was acquired by the newly formed Magnolia Petroleum Company. Upgrades and expansions of the refinery and pumping stations followed. By the mid-1920s, Magnolia operated refineries in Beaumont, Fort Worth, and Corsicana. Socony took control of Magnolia in 1925. In 1951, Socony and Vacuum merged; in 1959, the name was changed to Mobil.

The first local refinery workers' labor union was chartered in May 1913 in Beaumont. The Magnolia workers staged a two-week strike during the summer of 1918. This was the first time a refinery was shut down by a labor union. The workers gained a 5¢-per-hour pay increase. The refinery was the largest employer in Beaumont by 1920.

Replying to your communication, KFDM is a Western Electric 101-B Transmitter complete, operating on 306 meters. The Station is located atop the office building of the MAGNOLIA PETROLEUM COMPANY REFINERY AT BEAUMONT TEXAS, WHERE THE CELEBRATED LINE OF MAGNOLENE LUBRICANTS GREASES GASOLINE AND WAXES ARE MANUFACTURED. We are pleased if you enjoyed the program and thank you for your applause.
Yours sincerely,
MAGNOLIA PETROLEUM COMPANY.

Hitting the airwaves in October 1924, KFDM ("Kall For Dependable Magnolene") was the Magnolia refinery's radio station. Assistant superintendent John "Magnolene Mike" Newton and company dentist Dr. Harry Cloud managed the radio station, with Cloud also directing the station's band. Magnolene was the brand name for the company's motor oil. The reverse of this postcard states, "We expect to Radiocast a Programme every Tuesday and Friday, starting at 8 p.m. Central Standard Time, with a Sacred Concert every other Sunday evening at 9 p.m."

Joseph S. Cullinan (1860–1937) and Arnold Schlaet (1859–1946) formed the Texas Fuel Company on January 2, 1902. Former Texas governor James Hogg came on board soon after. Cullinan, Schlaet, and John "Bet-a-Million" Gates then formed an affiliate, the Producers Oil Company. The businessmen formed the Texas Company on May 1, 1902.

In August 1902, oil transported by pipeline from Spindletop to a planned refinery site near Port Arthur would be the first crude oil sold by the Texas Company. Four months later, construction began on a refinery, and the first refined product was produced on November 13, 1903. Port Arthur became the refinery and transportation center for Gulf Oil and the Texas Company.

37 500 Bbl. Oil Tank on fire, BEAUMONT, Tex.

BURNING TANK 35000 BARRELS.

BEAUMONT, TEXAS.

The early large oil storage tanks were 37,500-barrel tanks with a diameter of 94 feet and a height of 30 feet, and 55,000-barrel tanks with a diameter of 1,142 feet and a height of 30 feet. The Texas Company initially built a 37,500-barrel tank at Port Arthur and two more at Garrison Station, a mile and a half from Spindletop. Lightning strikes caused many oil-tank fires in the early years.

Some early postcards were "generically" produced and captioned with different geographic locations. This view of a burning oil tank may hold the record: 64 different printings, attributed to 15 different cities (including Beaumont) in five different states! The consensus of several historians is that the actual location is near Olean, New York, and that the photographer is Frank Robbins of Pennsylvania. (Victoria Manning.)

FLAGSHIP OF THE TEXAS COMPANY'S FLEET OF OIL CARRYING VESSELS, THE "TEXAS" FINEST AND MOST MODERN OCEAN-GOING OIL CARRIER IN THE WORLD, LAUNCHED AT NEWPORT NEWS, VIRGINIA ON SAN JACINTO DAY, APRIL 21ST, 1908. LENGTH 410 FEET, BEAM 52 FEET, CAPACITY 8,000 TONS OR EQUIVALENT TO OVER 50,000 BARRELS.

The Texas Company's flagship, the *Texas*, was launched at Newport News, Virginia, on April 21, 1908. The postcard caption describes this early oil tanker as the "finest and most modern ocean-going oil carrier in the world," with a capacity of 50,000 barrels of oil.

HIGGINS OIL & FUEL CO'S STORAGE TANKS, BEAUMONT, TEXAS.
These groups, consisting of 24 Steel Tanks of 37,500 barrels capacity each, are painted with
"*CARBONIZING COATING.*"
Manufactured only by THE GOHEEN MANUFACTURING CO., Canton, O., U. S. A.

In this advertisement, the Goheen Manufacturing Company of Canton, Ohio, depicts several Higgins Oil & Fuel Company storage tanks near Beaumont. Patillo Higgins, with some Beaumont businessmen, formed the Higgins Oil & Fuel Company just months after the Lucas discovery well. On April 18, 1901, the company completed the first of several oil gushers at Spindletop. After several of Higgins's partners sold their interest to the Houston Oil Company, Higgins reluctantly did the same.

John Warne "Bet-a-Million" Gates (1855–1911) worked his way from a barbed-wire salesman to the cofounder of a major barbed wire manufacturing and distribution company. One of the founders of the Texas Company, Gates was a shrewd investor, an avid gambler, and a philanthropist. Flags in Port Arthur and on Texas Company ships flew at half-staff at his death.

Beaumont's Crosby House was built in 1879. During the Spindletop boom days, it became known as the Crosby Hotel and was a popular location for oilmen to meet. One author described the oil-trading at the Crosby as "the center of the madness." The hotel was remodeled in 1888, 1903, and 1930. This postcard shows the hotel after the last remodeling. The original hotel was constructed of wood. The hotel was demolished in 1977.

Beaumont's Keith Park was established by the city with a nine-acre land purchase on April 14, 1931. The park was named after Alice Carroll Keith, wife of lumberman and oilman Jehu Frank Keith (1857–1921). After making a fortune in the lumber business, Keith was fortunate to have some of the early Spindletop wells on his land. Alice carried on the family's philanthropic endeavors after J. Frank's death.

The second Spindletop oil boom, or "New Spindletop," began in 1925 with the completion of Yount-Lee Oil's No. 2 McFaddin well. The well tested 1,500 barrels of oil per day from a depth of 2,517 feet. During the next few years, Yount-Lee dominated the field's deeper flank drilling. The Yount-Lee Oil Company was purchased by the Stanolind Oil Company for $41.8 million in 1935, then the third-largest cash transaction in American business history.

The Yount-Lee Oil Company drilled many wells at Spindletop during the late 1920s and early 1930s. The wreckage of its No. 29 McFaddin on May 5, 1927, shows how dangerous working on these early derricks could be. Men inspect the remains of the derrick and the twisted pipe of this Yount-Lee well. (Texas Energy Museum, Beaumont, Texas.)

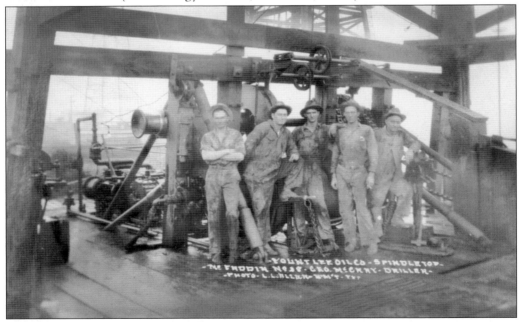

L.L. Allen was an active photographer in the early Texas Gulf Coast oil fields, and his photographs often included views of a rig's drilling crew. On the reverse of this postcard is written, "Spindletop oil field in 1927. Geo. McCray—driller with his crew of roughnecks." (Texas Energy Museum, Beaumont, Texas.)

This oil-well fire has been identified as a Rio Bravo Oil Company well, drilled during the second Spindletop oil boom. Rio Bravo Oil Company, owned by the Southern Pacific Railroad, drilled and completed many high-rate oil wells on Southern Pacific's railroad track easement at Spindletop. In the first five years of production, deeper flank wells at Spindletop produced more than 59 million barrels of oil.

Capt. W.C. Tyrell (1847–1924) joined with the four Heywood brothers to form the Heywood Oil Company in 1901. Tyrell served as president of the highly successful company. As a major financier in Beaumont, he also successfully invested in real estate and the rice industry. In 1923, he donated the old First Baptist Church building to the city. The building became the Tyrell Library in 1926.

80   BURNING OIL WELL, BEAUMONT, TEXAS

Tyrrell Public Library, Beaumont, Texas

151-30-N

The "Golden Triangle" is formed by connecting the cities of Beaumont, Orange, and Port Arthur. This area has a large concentration of oil refineries and petrochemical plants, as well as other industries attracted to the area's access to the Gulf of Mexico.

World's Largest Petroleum Butadiene Plant
PORT NECHES, NEAR PORT ARTHUR & ORANGE, TEXAS

Butadiene is a significant ingredient in synthetic rubber. During World War II, the federal government built a 100,000-ton butadiene plant near the eastern Jefferson County town of Port Neches, 15 miles south of Beaumont. Involved in the planning and building was a "technical committee" from five oil companies: Gulf Oil, the Texas Company, Atlantic Refining, Pure Oil, and Socony-Vacuum Oil. In 1955, the plant was sold to Goodrich-Gulf and Texas US Chemical.

OIL FIELDS, ORANGE, TEXAS   H-329

The Orange oil field is located 25 miles east of Beaumont, just west of the town of Orange. Gas seepages into water wells and sulphur springs led oil prospectors to the area. Between 1903 and 1913, several wells were drilled without a commercial discovery. The Rio Bravo Oil Company completed the field's discovery well, the No. 1 Bland, in August 1913. The well produced 150–300 barrels of oil per day and, at the time, was the deepest oil production in the state.

LITTLE SIX GUSHER
ORANGE · TEXAS

The Little Six Oil Company completed a 50-barrel-per-day well in 1920 in what would be the most active area of drilling in the Orange field. This No. 1 Chesson well set off active drilling for the next two years, including the field's first oil gusher, the Edgerly Petroleum Company's No. 1 Carbello, which tested between 3,000 and 5,500 barrels of oil per day.

The Brownie-Babette Oil Company, based in Orange, Texas, filed its company charter between 1912 and 1914. The company completed five oil wells in the Orange oil field between 1922 and 1935. Its No. 8 McLean, whose wreckage is shown here with a "blowout" date of September 5, 1922, was eventually completed as a 350-barrel-a-day oil well in May 1923.

Edgerly Petroleum filed its company charter on March 22, 1915. The company was also an active operator in southwest Louisiana, including the Vinton (Ged) oil field of nearby Calcasieu Parish. By May 1921, the company was the third-highest oil producer in the Orange field, behind Gulf Production Company and Humble Oil & Refining Company. The wreckage shown here, dated March 25, 1926, and attributed to a spring storm, is of one of Edgerly's derricks in the Orange field.

Two

THE TEXAS GULF COAST

The Saratoga Oil & Pipe Line Company drilled two significant wells near Saratoga, in Hardin County. In the fall of 1901, the Hooks No. 1 reached a total depth of 995 feet, testing oil at intermittent rates of 25–100 barrels of oil per day. The Hooks No. 2 was completed in March 1902, testing at rates of up to 500 barrels per day.

Drilling occurred at a rapid pace for the next few years. Saratoga's peak production, in 1905, was approximately 3.1 million barrels of oil. As with the other early Hardin County fields, Saratoga was proven to be underlain by a salt dome, with the top of salt at approximately 1,900 feet below the surface.

VIEW IN OIL FIELDS, SOUR LAKE, TEXAS.

In 1895, the Savage brothers drilled several shallow wells near Sour Lake in Hardin County, producing low oil rates. In 1898, the Gulf Coast Refining Company signed a contract with the Savage brothers, committing to construct a small refinery. The business venture ended when the brothers could not provide enough oil. Sour Lake oil field is underlain by salt, penetrated as shallow as 720 feet.

Waste Oil Fire, Sour Lake, Texas

Sour Lake's first oil gusher, in 1902, at the Atlantic & Pacific Company's well, flowed more than 10,000 barrels of oil per day from a depth of 656 feet. Several wells were completed in 1902, with rates between 500 and 10,000 barrels per day. Sour Lake quickly became an oil boomtown. A fire on August 24, 1903, destroyed several derricks and much oil field equipment.

BATSON OIL FIELD

On October 31, 1903, the Paraffine Oil Company completed its No. 1 Fee well, a 600-barrel-per-day oil well from a depth of 790 feet. The well was located near Batson, in Hardin County. A few months later, the company's No. 3 well came in as a 15,000-barrel-per-day gusher. Batson oil field produced 10 million barrels in 1904.

By 1905, an oil pipeline connected Batson, Saratoga, and Sour Lake oil fields to the Beaumont area oil refineries. This pipeline crew in the Piney Woods/Big Thicket area of East Texas appears to be made up of black workers. The Texas Company laid a pipeline from Sour Lake to the company's Port Neches refinery.

LAYING PIPE LINE THROUGH PINEY WOODS
EASTERN TEXAS FOR THE TEXAS COMPANY

The town of Humble was named for Pleasant Smith Humble, who opened the first post office in the area in 1886 and later became a justice of the peace. In 1909, Ross Sterling purchased two producing wells and acquired leases in the area. In January 1911, he joined with five businessmen to incorporate the Humble Oil Company, named after the nearby town, with $150,000 of capital. (Humble Museum, Humble, Texas.)

Main Street, Humble, Texas.

MOONSHINE HILL, HUMBLE, TEXAS.

Moonshine Hill, an elongated topographic feature rising approximately 20 feet above the surrounding area, is associated with the center of the Humble oil field. George Hart drilled two unsuccessful wells in 1902. C.E. Barrett drilled several wells in 1904, some of which were gas blowouts. In October 1904, the Higgins Oil & Fuel Company drilled and completed a gas well a half-mile southeast of the Barrett wells. (Humble Museum, Humble, Texas.)

Blow-out in Oil Field at Humble, Texas.

During the early years of drilling at Humble, there were many gas blowouts. This was due to several high-pressure gas zones between the depths of 600 and 900 feet that had to be drilled through on the way to the deeper oil zones. The Higgins Oil & Fuel Company No. 2 well is often mentioned as an early "gasser" or "miniature volcano" that erupted with gas, water, sand, and shale.

GUSHER IN OIL FIELD, HUMBLE, TEXAS, NEAR HOUSTON.

877

The start of the Humble oil boom began with the D.R. Beatty No. 2 Fee well, completed from a depth of 700 feet. The well, completed in January 1905, flowed 8,500 barrels of oil per day. Within two months of the Beatty well's completion, the field was producing 90,000 barrels of oil per day. After three months, the field boasted 28 oil gushers and had produced three million barrels of oil.

One of the earliest references to Moonshine Hill was the Moonshine Air Jammer Company's oil-pumping station, which started operation in 1905. Initially, Moonshine Hill consisted of tents and shacks housing the oil field workers. By 1909, Moonshine Hill included a grocery store, a school, and several saloons. The F.P. (Farmers Petroleum) Company maintained an air plant, shown here around 1915, near Moonshine Hill.

MOONSHINE AIR PLANT, LARGEST IN THE WORLD, OIL FIELD, HUMBLE, TEXAS. NEAR HOUSTON.

Earthern Oil Tanks at Humble, Tex.

Due to a lack of oil-storage tanks and the high volumes of associated produced water, sand, and silt, the Guffey Company used large, open earthen tanks as settling tanks and for oil storage. Visible in this postcard are five open earthen storage tanks, several large wooden storage tanks, and more than 20 wooden derricks. In 1905, the Humble field produced 15.6 million barrels of oil, the peak year for the oil field.

GUFFEY CO'S GROUND STORAGE TANKS, HUMBLE, TEXAS.   8781
TANK IN FOREGROUND CONTAINS AN ACTUAL AREA OF ABOUT 40 ACRES AND CONTAINS ABOUT
3 500 000 BARRELS OF OIL.

This Guffey Company's 40-acre operation held over 3.5 million barrels of oil. Other photographs at Humble show a wooden cover or "roof" over some of the earthen tanks. By early 1906, the Humble oil field led the Texas Gulf Coast with more than 6 million barrels of oil stored in earthen tanks. During 1915, the Farmers Petroleum Company had four wells pumping as much as 50,000 barrels of oil per day into an earthen storage tank.

GREAT TEXAS OIL FIRE,
HUMBLE, TEX., JULY 23, 1905.
BURNING 12 TANKS HAVING AN AREA
OF 4 ACRES EACH, WITH CAPACITY OF
235000 BARRELS EACH, TOTAL AREA
BURNT 100 ACRES WITH ABOUT
2500000 BARRELS OF OIL
CONSUMED IN FIRE.

8777

THE SIMMS GUSHER, THE LARGEST GUSHER IN THE U. S.
50 THOUSAND BARRELS PER DAY, OIL FIELDS,
HUMBLE, TEXAS, NEAR HOUSTON.

A July 23, 1905, lightning strike ignited the Texas Company's oil storage at Humble. The "Great Texas Oil Fire" destroyed 12 open earthen tanks with a capacity of 235,000 barrels each. The fire consumed an estimated 2.5 million barrels of oil. More than 200 men with 75 mules struggled to construct earthen embankments to contain the burning oil. Between 50 and 60 men and many mules perished.

E.F. Simms claimed to have "the largest gusher in the U.S." at a rate of 50,000 barrels per day. The company drilled and completed this well, with a rate of 14,000 barrels of oil per day. The next day, the Producers Oil Company purchased the well. There is no confirmation that any Humble well reached daily rates approaching 50,000 barrels. A note on the reverse of this postcard reads, "This is where oil flows as free as water. That's the stuff that made John D. [Rockefeller] the King of the World."

OIL FIELD, HUMBLE, TEXAS. NEAR HOUSTON.

E. C. KROPP, PUBL. MILWAUKEE. NO. 1026

Mule- or horse-drawn wagons transported pipe and oil field supplies to the early Texas oil fields. From 1905 to 1913, the drilling at Humble was into the salt dome's caprock, predominantly composed of limestone. The caprock was encountered as shallow as 700 feet and the salt as shallow as 1,214 feet. Rotary tools drilled from the surface to the top of the caprock, where casing was set. Cable tools drilled the remainder of the well.

In 1906, an early theory explaining oil gushers involved the Humble oil field. The presence of underground oil "veins," analogous to the veins or arteries in the human body, were "surveyed" in late 1904. The conclusion was that the higher-rate oil gushers were associated with areas of "compound" or "main arteries." The study claimed success in predicting several wells using this (short-lived) theory!

OIL WELL, HUMBLE, TEXAS, NEAR HOUSTON.

A Merry Christmas & a Happy New Year from us Tholzdast

C. KROPP CO., MILWAUKEE.

Early oil-storage tanks were constructed of wood, but these were quickly replaced with larger steel tanks. At Humble, 55,000-barrel storage tanks were the most common size. By 1917, the Producers Oil Company had built 10 steel tanks of this size at Humble. (Humble Museum, Humble, Texas.)

OIL FIELDS (UPPER).
MUD RESERVOIRS, BUTLER TRACT NEW DEV.
(LOWER), HUMBLE, TEXAS.

The Butler subdivision, located on the northwest portion of the Humble oil field, saw drilling on small tracts in 1915 and 1916. During 1915, several oil gushers were drilled on the Stephenson and Landslide leases from depths of 2,900 to 3,300 feet. The field produced more than 11 million barrels of oil in 1915 and over 10 million barrels the following year. In 1915, Humble was the highest-producing oil field in the Texas Gulf Coast.

961   PARTIAL VIEW OF TEXAS PIPE LINE COMPANY'S TANK FARM, HUMBLE, TEXAS

The Texas Company operated a pipeline pump station and tank farm near Moonshine Hill. On December 21, 1902, TEXACO was first used as a product name. The name, which came from the telegraph address of the Texas Company's New York office, became a registered trademark in 1906. The company first used the red star and green "T" trademark in 1909. (Humble Museum, Humble, Texas.)

Humble oil production had dropped considerably in 1906 and 1907. The next year, though, saw a rebound, with eight new wells producing more than 1,000 barrels of oil per day and 28 wells producing more than 500 barrels of oil per day. A note on the reverse of this postcard reads, "Papa. This the way an oil gusher looks in Humble. This is a greasy town, alright to visit, but not to live in. I had my picture taken on a derrick (8-24-1909)."

Oil Gusher, Humble, Texas.

Big Gusher in the oilfield of Goose Creek, Tex.

This card for sale at "The Big Star" only

Rejuvenating the field, the Producers Oil Company completed its No. 11 Carroll, which produced at a rate of 10,000 barrels of oil per day, in deeper sands on the east side of the field in November 1908. Other active companies at Humble were the Gulf Production Company, Invincible Oil Company, Mud Lake Oil Company, Satsuma Oil Company, Deep Shale Oil Company, and Deep Sand Oil Company. (Humble Museum, Humble, Texas.)

As early as 1906, fishermen reported gas bubbling in the waters of Tabbs Bay, in eastern Harris County. Just onshore, there were also gas seeps. John Galliard contracted for the drilling of a well on his property. The well blew in on August 23, 1916, at 8,100 barrels of oil per day. This well and others drilled that year began the Goose Creek oil boom.

The Hoffman Deep Well Company was capitalized at $100,000 and held a 25-acre Gaillard lease and a 25-acre Ashbel Smith lease at Goose Creek. Its No. 2 "Gailard" (Gaillard) oil gusher blew in on July 13, 1916 (right). The company's No. 2 "Ashbell" (Ashbel) Smith was also drilled in 1916 (below). Additional drilling at Goose Creek resulted in 1916 production of 42,000 barrels of oil.

By February 1917, over a dozen oil operators were active at Goose Creek (above), including Sun Company, E.F. Simms, Houston Deep Well Oil Company, Empire Gas and Fuel, Magnolia Petroleum Company, Gulf Production Company, Producers Oil Company, and Blaffer and Farish. The Blaffer–Farish partnership would later become part of Humble Oil Company,

and both men would serve as company directors. Humble built wooden oil storage tanks near Baytown, which were later replaced by larger steel tanks (below). Frank G. Allen (1881–1921) was a prolific photographer in several Texas Gulf Coast oil fields. (Texas Energy Museum, Beaumont, Texas.)

NERY. BAY TOWN TEX. Photo By. F. G. Allen. HOUSTON TEX.

"SWEET EVANGELINE".

Photo by Schlueter

GOOSE CREEK, NEAR HOUSTON, TEXAS. 35,000 BBLS. PER DAY.

Frank J. Schlueter (1874–1972) took the original photograph of Goose Creek's "Sweet Evangeline," the 35,000–barrel–a–day gusher. Schlueter and his wife opened a studio in Houston in 1907. Well known for his oil field photographs, he also chronicled other industries and events in the Houston and Texas City areas. The well shown here is probably the Simms-Sinclair No. 11 Sweet, completed on August 4, 1917.

In 1917, oil leases were going for high prices, including a five-acre tract that leased for $75,000. Leasing could be a challenge. When Humble Oil attempted to secure one lease, the landowner insisted on a clause whereby the lease could be cancelled if gates were left open and his cows got out. The old Goose Creek townsite, near the bay shore, was relocated three-quarters of a mile from the water.

Main Street of Goose Creek, Tex.

MITCHELL-MITCHELL & STEPHENSON GENERAL MERCHANDISE

BA COFFEE

This card for sale at "The Big Star" only.

44

In 1918, Humble Oil completed one of the most impressive oil gushers in the field, with a little bit of luck. A roughneck on the well, intending to perforate the casing at 3,000 feet, mistakenly did so at 2,300 feet. The well was a 20,000-barrel-a-day gusher. To support the war effort, in 1918, the Goose Creek oil field produced approximately nine million barrels of oil.

In June 1918, Humble Oil began purchasing land near Goose Creek for the construction of an oil refinery. As the construction began in early 1919, the area experienced "one hundred days straight of rain" and "clouds of flies and malaria-carrying mosquitos, grasshoppers, office-invading snakes, and bellicose Brahman bulls." The refinery, which began operations in 1920, employed 100 workers and processed 10,000 barrels of crude oil per day.

Humble Oil Co., Goose Creek and Baytown, Texas

Humble Community House
BAYTOWN, TEXAS

Texas Gulf Coast Oil Well
TRI CITY AREA NEAR
BAYTOWN AND GOOSE CREEK, TEXAS

To house its workers, Humble initially used army tents and barracks, feeding them at an old farmhouse. Later, bunkhouses and mess halls were built. Humble eventually helped workers purchase their own homes in Baytown. The Humble Community House (1924–1963) hosted movies, dances, lectures, recitals, and receptions for the workers and their families.

In 1918, Humble Oil and Gulf Production companies drilled the first offshore wells at Goose Creek. This was the first offshore drilling in the state of Texas. Ships and tankers maneuvered around the offshore wells that soon covered Tabbs Bay. Humble built docks and loading facilities to service its refinery.

46

Goose Creek flows into the Houston Ship Channel, which provides access to the Gulf of Mexico. The channel proved an attractive location for oil refineries, and by 1930, there were nine refineries along the channel. John Wayne's role as Chance Buckman in *Hellfighters* (1969) was patterned after real-life oil field firefighter Paul "Red" Adair (1915–2004). Parts of the movie were filmed in the Goose Creek oil field.

Damon Mound is located in Brazoria County, 12 miles north of the West Columbia oil field. The prominent mound, associated with an underlying salt dome, was first drilled in 1901 by J.M Guffey, but oil production was not established until 1915 by the Texas Exploration Company. The Cumings Drugstore in Rosenberg, 20 miles north, may have been where this postcard was sold. (Susan Davidek Svec collection.)

In 1917, the Tyndall-Wyoming Oil & Development Company completed the No. 1 Hogg (Japhet) well at 10 barrels of oil per day, followed by a 200-barrel-a-day well. Larger oil companies, including Humble, Texas Company, and Gulf Production quickly entered the

The Pierce Junction oil field is located one mile south of the Houston Astrodome. The area's surface gas seeps, similar to Spindletop, led to the drilling of a well in 1901, which encountered

field, drilling and completing many high-rate wells. During much of 1922, West Columbia produced at the highest daily oil rate of any Texas Gulf Coast oil field. (Texas Energy Museum, Beaumont, Texas.)

shows of oil. The 1921 Gulf No. 2 Taylor is generally considered the discovery well for the field. This photograph of the Gulf camp shows workers' housing, a café, and several oil derricks.

West Columbia is located in Brazoria County, approximately 50 miles southwest of Houston. As with other salt domes, surface features such as a low mound and oil and gas seeps attracted oilmen to the area soon after Spindletop's 1901 discovery. The first well at West Columbia was drilled in late 1901, and several wells, some of which encountered gas or shows of oil, were drilled in the following years.

The Texas Pipe Line Company operated its Arnold oil–pumping station, named for the Arnold lease, as well as a large oil storage tank farm, at West Columbia. Offices and company barracks were provided for the employees. To help avoid some of the issues experienced during other Texas oil booms, company management forbade gambling at the West Columbia camp.

Former Texas governor James Hogg (1851–1906) purchased a plantation near West Columbia as an investment and second home. Hogg's will required that the mineral rights be retained for 15 years after his death. With the discovery of oil at West Columbia, Hogg's children became very wealthy and shared their wealth through the Hogg Foundation.

Success at the Markham salt dome occurred on June 5, 1908, with the completion of the Hardy Oil No. 1 Hudson well. The well initially tested between 1,500 and 3,000 barrels of oil per day, but within six months, had dropped to 150 barrels of oil per day. The well shown in this photograph, dated June 6, 1908, is probably the Hardy well, though the oil rate is listed at 4,000 barrels of oil per day. (Matagorda County Museum, Bay City, Texas.)

Clemville is located approximately five miles northwest of Markham, in Matagorda County. F.J. Hardy and W.C. Moore chose the area for drilling near a gas seep. This was the discovery well for the Markham oil field. A small community sprang up, initially known as Hardy. F.J. Hardy sold his interests to F.J. Clemenger, who, along with R.H. Danner, further developed the oil field. The community was renamed Clemville and grew rapidly as a boomtown. The derricks shown in these photographs are on the Rosen lease near Clemville. (Matagorda County Museum, Bay City, Texas.)

In 1902, a well at Matagorda County's Big Hill encountered shallow gas. Subsequent drilling discovered oil. Sulphur occurred in the salt dome's shallow limestone caprock. In 1909, the Gulf Sulphur Company was founded. It was reorganized in 1916 as Texas Gulf Sulphur. The US government encouraged the company to build a sulphur-processing plant to aid the war effort. Construction began in August 1918, with first production in March 1919.

In 1926, gas was discovered 60 miles northwest of Houston in Austin County, east of the town of Bellville. This was followed in 1928 by Humble Oil's 500-barrel-a-day Gutowsky well. In this photograph, a Humble Oil & Refining Company drilling crew poses in front of the C-2 Grawunder well, drilled on the west flank of the Raccoon Bend oil field in 1929. The driller is identified as W.C. Whatley.

Hauling Crude Oil for fuel from the supply tanks in El Campo to the rice farms.

Oil Well, Hamman Field, Bay City, Texas

El Campo is located in Wharton County, approximately 75 miles southwest of Houston. Rice farming has been a large part of the area's economy. As early as 1904, drilling for oil occurred in the county, and the first commercial oil production was located near Boling in 1925. Boling's streets are named after oil companies, such as Gulf, Humble, Magnolia, and Sun. Sulphur was produced at the Boling salt dome from 1927 to 1993.

The Hamman oil field, near Bay City in Matagorda County, was discovered in 1934. The Hamman family has been involved in the oil and refining business for four generations. William H. Hamman (1830–1890) leased acreage in what would later be parts of Spindletop, Saratoga, and Sour Lake oil fields. Hamman Oil & Refining Company also operated a refinery on the south side of Bay City.

Chalmers was located approximately five miles north of Bay City. The Shelly Oil Company operated a refinery there at least as early as 1936. In 1938, it was the smallest of 18 refineries in the Texas Gulf Coast, with a capacity of 1,000 barrels per day. The refinery is listed in the 1945 Bay City Chamber of Commerce Directory as is the Hamman refinery.

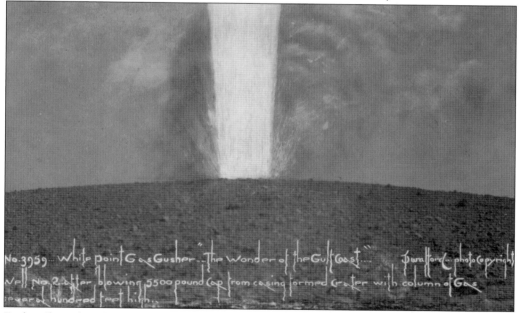

Early oil exploration around Corpus Christi occurred near gas seeps on the White Point peninsula. In 1907, the first of many gas blowouts took place. The White Point Gas gusher blew out in January 1916, with a "several hundred feet high" column of gas. It was reported that the roaring gas could be heard for seven miles. "The Wonder of the Gulf Coast" well is noted on this postcard as the J.M Guffey No. 2 well.

THE FAMOUS GUFEY GAS WELL, CORRUS CHRISTI, TEXAS.

The J.M. Guffey Petroleum Company had the misfortune to drill several gas blowouts in the White Point area without finding oil. Some sources suggest that the company's No. 1 well was junked and abandoned, and the derrick skidded over to drill the No. 2, which became the famous gas blowout. Other sources mention the No. 1 well as a gas blowout. (Dan Kilgore Papers, Special Collections and Archives, Texas A&M University–Corpus Christi, Bell Library.)

"All that remains to be seen of Guffey well No. 1" is a crater. The well, which actually may be well No. 2, flowed at an estimated rate of 50–100 million cubic feet of gas per day before igniting. The fire reportedly could be seen for over 100 miles. When the fire finally burned itself out, it left a crater 200 feet wide by 100 feet deep. (Dan Kilgore Papers, Special Collections and Archives, Texas A&M University–Corpus Christi, Bell Library.)

No 3979 At White Point Texas.
All that remains to be seen of Guffey Well No. 1

During 1922, the Moody–Seagraves Company drilled four wells in the Corpus Christi area. Perhaps the "Old Seagraves" burning mound was one of the company's wells. There were 30 blowouts in Saxet Field, located eight miles west of Corpus Christi. On August 16, 1930, the first oil well in the field, the Saxet Gas Company No. 6 Dunn, was completed at a rate of 500 barrels of oil per day.

Though oil and gas had been discovered in the onshore area around Corpus Christi decades earlier, the first drilling in the Texas state waters of Corpus Christi Bay did not occur until 1950. Barge drilling rigs were equipped to drill in the shallow waters with an average depth of 10 feet.

"Old Seagraves", Corpus Christi, Texas

First Major Blow Out - Still Active

In January 1933, the Standard Oil Company of Kansas drilled its No. 1 Madeley well in the Conroe oil field. The gusher immediately caught fire. The well burned for three months, and the smoke could be seen in Houston, 35 miles to the south. A huge burning crater formed at the well site. Workers extinguished the fire by drilling a directional relief well and pumping mud into the wellbore.

George W. Strake completed the Conroe oil field's discovery well, the No. 1 South Texas Development Company, in December 1931. Between August 1932 and December 1933, there were 12 blowouts in the Conroe oil field. The Standard Oil Company of Kansas No. 2 Madeley well blew out just nine days after its No. 1 blowout.

The first commercial oil well in Hidalgo County was the Otto C. Woods, et al., No. 1 John Lawrence, completed on September 18, 1934. This well opened the Sam Fordyce (or Samforydce) oil field, located less than 10 miles from the Rio Grande River. The well tested at over 1,000 barrels of oil per day. Initially, the oil was stored in an earthen pit near the well.

Texas City is located 35 miles southeast of Houston. On April 16, 1947, ammonium nitrate fertilizer exploded on the French ship *Grandcamp*. The fire spread to the freighter SS *High Flyer* the following day. The death toll was 581, with more than 5,000 injured. Severe damage occurred at Humble Pipe Line Company's tank farm and at facilities of the Republic Oil Refining Company, Stone Oil Company, Sid Richardson Refining Company, and Pan American Refining Company.

The Texas Company Building, Houston, Tex.

In 1908, the general office of the Texas Oil Company was moved from Beaumont to Houston. The Texas Company Building was designed by noted New York architects Whitney Warren and Charles Wetmore. Excavation began in 1914, and the 13-story building on the corner of San Jacinto Street and Rusk Avenue was completed in 1915.

Gulf Building, Houston, Texas

The 36-story Gulf Building, at Main Street and Rusk Avenue, was completed in 1929. Until 1931, it was the tallest building west of the Mississippi River, and from 1929 to 1963, it was the tallest building in Houston. From 1966 to 1974, the "Gulf Lollipop"—a large rotating orange porcelain Gulf insignia—adorned the rooftop. In 2000, the building was renamed the J.P. Morgan Chase Bank Building.

The 32-story Niels Esperson Building (right), at Rusk and Travis Streets, opened in 1927 as the tallest structure in Texas. Mellie Keenan Esperson (c. 1870–1945), wife of Niels, oversaw the construction of the building based on designs commissioned by her husband before his death in 1922. Niels studied geology in California, explored for oil in Oklahoma and Kansas, and acquired much of his wealth in the Humble oil field. In 1941, the adjoining 19-story Mellie Esperspon Building was completed.

Construction of Houston's Shamrock Hotel, the project of noted oilman Glenn H. McCarthy, began in 1946. The 18-story, 1,100-room hotel was completed in 1949 at an estimated cost of $21 million. The Shamrock, which provided the inspiration for the hotel Conquistador in the 1956 movie *Giant*, was demolished in 1987.

Continental Oil Company (Conoco) moved its corporate headquarters from Ponca City, Oklahoma, to Houston in 1949–1950. Its downtown offices were in the seven-story Oil and Gas Building on Lamar Street (shown here). This building was completed in 1937 and demolished in 1971. In 1956, the company moved to the Conoco Building at 1300 Main Street. Conoco, Inc. and Phillips Petroleum merged in 2002. The ConocoPhillips corporate headquarters is now in west Houston.

Humble Oil Company relocated from Humble, Texas, to Houston in 1912. In 1921, Humble moved into a nine-story building at Main and Polk Streets. In 1935, the 15-story Humble Tower was added, followed in 1940 by another smaller addition. In 1963, Humble moved into a new 45-story building (shown here) at 800 Bell Street. The Petroleum Club of Houston moved from the Rice Hotel to the 43rd and 44th floors of the Humble (now Exxon Mobil) Building in 1963.

Three

NORTH TEXAS AND THE PANHANDLE

The discovery of oil and gas near Amarillo, in the Texas Panhandle, brought many oil companies to the area, including larger firms, such as Gulf, the Texas Company, Magnolia, and Roxana (Shell). After the discovery of gas by the Masterson No. 1 well in 1918, Amarillo Oil Company drilled additional wells on the Masterson lease. By March 1920, the company's first four wells were producing at a combined rate of 160 million cubic feet of gas per day.

In 1901, a farmer struck oil at a depth of 263 feet while drilling for water in Petrolia, 15 miles east of Wichita Falls in Clay County. The towns of Oil City and Petrolia sprang up in the area, with Petrolia, nearer to the railroad, eventually winning out. The town and the nearby oil field were named for the oil town of Petrolia, Pennsylvania. By 1905, Petrolia was a boomtown.

296 Laying 16-inch Natural Gas Pipe Line from Henrietta to Dallas and Fort Worth, Texas.

Abundant natural gas was discovered at shallow depths near Petrolia in 1907. The Lone Star Gas Company, formed in 1909, provided gas to several communities. A 16-inch gas pipeline was laid through Henrietta to the Dallas–Fort Worth area, and two smaller gas pipelines were laid to Wichita Falls. Petrolia's estimated annual gas sales between the years 1915 and 1919 were 7–10 billion cubic feet.

PETROLIA GAS WELL.

Helium was also produced at Petrolia. The US Army built the nation's first helium-extraction plant at Petrolia in 1915. The same year, the cities of Dallas and Fort Worth, which had come to heavily rely on Petrolia's gas, called for a study of gas supplies in all known Texas fields to determine if gas pipelines should be laid from Oklahoma to meet the growing demand for natural gas.

Electra Oil Fields, near Wichita Falls, Texas.

Copyrighted by A. J. Haddix

The town of Electra is located 15 miles northwest of Wichita Falls. The Waggoner family began ranching in Wichita County in the 1850s. When the railroad arrived in the 1880s, the Waggoners convinced the railroad to build a switch at a location originally called Waggoner, later renamed Beaver or Beaver Switch. In 1902, the residents petitioned to change the town's name to Electra, in honor of W.T. Waggoner's daughter.

Oil Field. Electra. Tex 12-4-11   Photo by T Brady

Producers-Waggoner No 26 Electra Texas   Loden Foto

W.T. Waggoner, a local cattle baron, encountered oil in his ranch's water wells northwest of Petrolia as early as 1908. Though the oil added to his wealth, he initially complained that what he needed was water for his cattle. The Producers Oil Company, a subsidiary of the Texas Company, completed the No. 5 Waggoner well, at 50 barrels of oil per day, on January 17, 1911.

The Producers Oil Company drilled many wells on the Waggoner ranch. The No. 26 Waggoner well, shown here, was drilled in 1912. By early 1915, the company had drilled 76 wells on the ranch, and by 1917, at least 130 wells. The discovery of oil near Electra set off exploration in the area, leading to several additional oil fields in the geologic area known as the Red River Uplift.

The Clayco Oil & Pipeline Company formed after the oil discovery at Petrolia. Its No. 1 Woodruff-Putnam was the first oil gusher at Electra, blowing oil 100 feet into the air. When the well blew in on April 1, 1911, north of Electra, many citizens thought that the report was an April Fool's Day joke.

Churches often sponsored missions into the oil fields, and these 22 men, women, and children appear to be attending one. The note on the reverse of this postcard, postmarked 1913, mentions one of the early concerns at Electra: lack of good water. "Everybody here have to buy every drop of water they use. Get it from Vernon. Ship it in." The town of Vernon is 23 miles from Electra.

McBride-No. 1 Sheldon Lease. April 22nd 1912. Foto By Loden.

Baptist Oil Field Mission Electra Tex. Loden Foto

Producers Bickley No. 14 on Fire, Electra, Texas

The Producers Oil Company was a subsidiary of the Texas Company. This postcard of the company's No. 14 Bickley well burning bears a message on the reverse, expressing what was probably a common view of oil workers during a Texas summer: "Am working in the oil field in Texas. The weather is very warm." The postcard is postmarked July 23, 1913.

In this postcard's caption, "C.P. Co's." probably refers to the Corsicana Petroleum Company. In December 1915, the firm extended Electra field to the southwest with the completion of several oil wells. During the same year, the company built the first natural gasoline plant in Texas. Magnolia Petroleum Company purchased Corsicana Petroleum in 1925. The Texas Company's No. 240 oil tank's fire, ignited by a lightning strike on May 2, 1914, burned 55,000 barrels.

C. P. CO.'S 3700 BBL. TANK ON FIRE, ELECTRA, TEXAS.

Many of the early Electra oil field postcards bear the words "Loden Foto." Benjamin Harrison Loden (1871?–1926), according to his *Electra News* obituary, was a "pioneer photographer" and "the proprietor of the only studio in the city." On this postcard, the "d" has been reversed as a "b."

Wooden oil derricks with associated water tanks and boilers dotted the county's landscape. This Loden photograph of the Electra oil field shows a shack with a sign reading, "Prod. Oil Co. Stringer 24." The message on the reverse of this postcard describes some of the dangers working in the oil field: "I got my head cut up so it had to be sewed up and my ear." This postcard is postmarked May 20, 1913.

Electra wells produced from sands as shallow as 80 to 90 feet. Additional oil sands were encountered at 580, 965, 1,035, and 1,900 feet. Initial rates generally ranged from 50 to 1,200 barrels of oil per day, and the oil sands were 10 to 30 feet thick. The strong-performing Clayco No. 3 Putnam well, initially tested at 1,600 barrels per day, was, nine months later, still producing 600 barrels of oil per day.

Due to lack of tankage, Clayco initially stored oil in a pond formed by damming up a creek. In 1912, the Texas Pipeline Company completed an eight-inch oil pipeline from Electra to Fort Worth and Dallas. The same year, Magnolia Pipeline Company completed its eight-inch line from Electra to Corsicana to Beaumont, and the Pierce-Fordyce Association completed oil pipelines to its Fort Worth refinery.

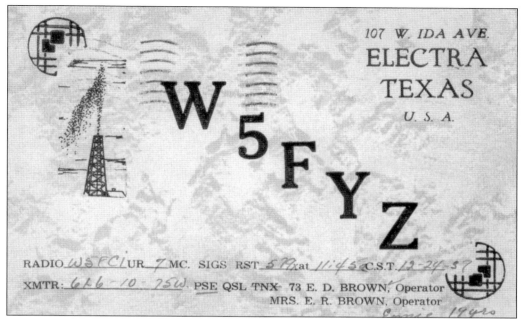

QSL postcards, exchanged by ham radio and CB operators, serve as confirmation receipts and usually list the radio frequency, date, time, and location. The cards often include a drawing or cachet, such as this gushing oil well from Electra. This postcard is dated and postmarked December 1937.

In 2001, the Texas Legislature declared Electra the "Pump Jack Capital of Texas." At that time, there were an estimated 5,000 pump jacks within a 10-mile radius of Electra, whose population was only 3,000! The town now holds its Pumping Jack Festival every April 1 to commemorate the April 1, 1911, Clayco oil gusher.

OIL FIELD, BURKBURNETT, TEXAS.

Burkburnett, in Wichita County, is 10 miles north of Wichita Falls. On July 18, 1912, Corsicana Oil Company completed the No. 1 Schmoker well for 75–85 barrels of oil per day from a depth of 1,837 feet. This well was three miles southwest of the town, in an area that would later be known as the "Burk" or "old Burk" oil pool.

Street Scene Residence Section, Burkburnett.
Sept 1920.

The Burkburnett oil field would reach national prominence during the summer of 1918. S.L. Fowler organized the Fowler Farm Oil Company and, on July 29, 1918, completed "Fowler's Folly" near the northeast edge of Burkburnett. The well tested at 2,200 barrels of oil per day from a depth of 1,784 feet. Before the success of the Fowler well, oil leases in the area were commonly acquired for as little as 25¢ per acre.

OIL TANKS AND WELLS, BURKBURNETT, TEXAS.

S.L. Fowler completed a second oil well and then sold his wells to Magnolia Petroleum Company for a hefty profit. This area became known as the Burkburnett Townsite oil pool. Town lots of an acre or less were leased. Within three weeks of the Fowler well completion, 56 rigs were working in the field, most on town lots. By the beginning of 1920, there were 1,200 wells on 1,500 acres.

Boomtown USA

Town lots initially leased for $1,000. Acre lots were commonly subdivided into half-acre tracts, and companies organized and sold stock based on holding these small tracts, offsetting a strong-producing well. The Townsite oil pool quickly reached production rates of over 50,000 barrels per day. By January 1919, there were 289 incorporated companies operating at Burkburnett. There were 168 flowing oil wells and 207 wells drilling. Acre leases were going for $15,000.

Boomtown USA

In April 1919, an area three miles northwest of Burkburnett proved to hold another large oil pool. The discovery well was either the Ryan Petroleum Company No. 1 R.M. (Bob) Waggoner, completed on April 17 at 4,800 barrels of oil per day, or the Burk-Waggoner Oil Company No. 1 Bob Waggoner, completed on April 26 or 29 at 2,750 barrels per day.

Beginning in April and throughout the summer of 1919, an area known as the "Northwest Extension," or the "Waggoner pool," saw rapid development, producing between 16,000 and 20,000 barrels of oil per day. By 1920, 885 wells had been drilled on 1,265 acres, or 1.4 acres per well. A study of the Townsite oil pool concluded that the oil could have been recovered just as effectively with only 250 wells, or about one well per five acres.

The Golden Cycle well was drilled in the Northwest Extension's Block 75. Early reports had the well "running a solid six-inch stream of oil" and being touted as the "greatest well yet discovered in the field." Initial flow rates were 5,000 barrels of oil per day. There are some images of the well on fire in April 1919.

Henry Hobbs and other Burkburnett businessmen formed the Texas Chief Oil & Gas Company in May 1919. The firm brought in several high-rate oil wells in the Northwest Extension area of Burkburnett, including a 5,000-barrel-per-day well known simply as the "Texas Chief." The well was located in Block 97 near the Red River, approximately three miles from the Golden Cycle well.

Text on image: FIGHTING THE FIRE IN OIL FIELD, BURKBURNETT, TEXAS.

As with many of the early oil fields, fires were not uncommon at Burkburnett. Four major oil field fires occurred within a few weeks during the fall of 1919. One fire destroyed two wells, a storage tank, trucks, and gathering lines valued at over $250,000 (in 1919 dollars). Another fire destroyed 19 storage tanks, for a loss of more than $300,000.

Text on image: CHAS. F. NOBLE OIL & GAS CO. BURKBURNETT-TEXAS. DERRICKS – BURKBURNETT, TEXAS. CASINGHEAD GASOLINE PLANT LARGEST IN THE WORLD 460x42. PIPE MATERIAL YARD. LOADING RACKS FOR TANK CARS. OFFICE. GARAGE.

Chas. F. Noble Oil & Gas Company of Tulsa, Oklahoma, operated a refinery, loading racks, a pipe yard, and a casinghead gasoline plant near Burkburnett. The company also completed oil wells in Blocks 85 and 86 of the Northwest Extension.

Lack of storage and an oversupply of oil necessitated the use of earthen oil tanks at Burkburnett until large storage tanks could be built. The construction of this 55,000-barrel tank, and, according to the caption, of 11 more tanks, indicates the rapid increase in oil production at Burkburnett.

Bradley's Corner in Wichita County, near the Red River, was one of many small towns that sprang up near Burkburnett after the discovery of oil. The short-lived community began with tents and shacks, then progressed to dining halls, saloons, and gambling houses. The town was abandoned after only a few years.

Fortunes were made and lost at Burkburnett. In October 1919, drilling at Burkburnett extended northwest of the Northwest Extension pool into the Red River, prompting a lawsuit between Texas and Oklahoma. This area became known as the "General" or "River" oil pool. The "Texhoma" of "Southeast Burkburnett" field was discovered southeast of town in October 1919.

One of the best-known oil field movies, *Boom Town*, starring, from left to right, Spencer Tracy, Hedy Lamarr, Claudette Colbert, and Clark Gable, hit theaters in 1940. A *Cosmopolitan* magazine article, "A Lady Comes to Burkburnett," was the inspiration for the movie. Promotional postcards featured the movie's four stars on the front and local theater information and advertisements on the reverse.

Borger is located in the Texas Panhandle's Hutchinson County, approximately 40 miles northeast of Amarillo. In March 1926, business partners Asa Phillip "Ace" Borger and John R. Miller purchased a 240-acre tract of land in the southern portion of the county. They recognized that recent nearby oil discoveries would bring thousands of people to the sparsely populated area. A town was laid out, and city and residential lots were sold.

In March 1925, the Borger oil field discovery well, the No. 1 Smith, came in producing 400 barrels of oil per day. In December, the No. 2 Smith came in at 3,000 barrels of oil per day. The No. 1 well was then reentered and deepened a few feet. On January 11, 1926, the well came in as a gusher at 7,000–10,000 barrels of oil per day.

More than 45,000 men and women rushed to the boomtown within the next few months. By October, the Panhandle & Santa Fe Railroad arrived, a post office was opened, and a school system was formed. Before the end of 1926, the town had telephone service, steam-generated electricity, a small hospital, and a newspaper. (Texas Energy Museum, Beaumont, Texas.)

Dixon Creek, a distributary of the Canadian River, runs through the Borger oil field. Many Borger oil field images refer to the area as the Dixon Creek Canyon. Wells were also drilled on pilings along the banks of the Canadian River. The McIlroy brothers formed the Dixon Creek Oil & Refining Company and built a refinery and a casinghead gas plant to process the large volumes of natural gas that were produced with the oil.

By June 1926, Phillips Oil and Dixon Creek Oil were the two top operators in the area, By September, there were 813 wells in the field, producing a total of 165,000 barrels of oil per day. Before the end of 1927, more than 20 oil companies were operating in the area, including Gulf, Magnolia, Marland, Plains, Skelly, and Prairie. Initially, due to a lack of railroads and pipelines, large oil storage tanks were constructed.

The massive wooden oil derricks of the early years were being replaced by steel derricks in the late 1920s and early 1930s. The town of Borger is visible in the background of this postcard, and railroad tank cars for transporting oil can be seen in the foreground at right.

"Shooting a well" involved using nitroglycerin to stimulate a well into production. The nitroglycerin was poured into a "torpedo," which was lowered into the well and detonated. An April 14, 1927, nitro-blast at the Anderson–Pritchard No. 1 Yahe well resulted in three deaths. Nitroglycerin was also used to extinguish oil field fires. Ward A. "Tex" Thornton (1891–1949), a well shooter, also made a name for himself as an oil-well firefighter in the Texas Panhandle.

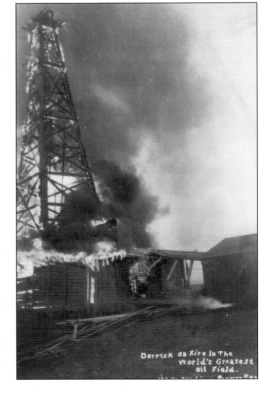

A Pantex-operated well, located one mile northeast of Borger near Whittenburg, caught fire while workers were pulling casing. One worker leaped to safety from the burning rig, though he and two other workers were treated for burns.

This card, postmarked 1927, includes a note: "This is a snap shot of how the 'black gold' does its stuff at times." Towns sprang up near Borger, though some lasted only months. Lots in Signal Hill, named after California's Signal Hill, began selling in May 1926; by the end of the year, the town had a population of approximately 10,000. By the end of the decade, the town was largely abandoned.

The oil fields near Borger had their share of poor road conditions. Oil derrick parts, pipe, and other equipment were best hauled by teams of horses, mules, or oxen. (Texas Energy Museum, Beaumont, Texas.)

OIL DERRICKS NIGHT SCENE
PAMPA TEXAS

Drilling a well is an around-the-clock operation, shown by these lights on a steel derrick in the 1950s. A note on the reverse on this postcard places this drilling operation "just outside the city limits" of Pampa, which is approximately 30 miles southeast of Borger.

Frank Phillips and his Oklahoma-based oil company decided to diversify and enter the refining business. The company's first refinery was built near Borger in 1927. Conoco and Phillips merged in 2002, and the company still operates a refinery at Borger. The refinery, with a capacity of 146,000 barrels per day, primarily processes medium-sour crude oil from West Texas, the Texas Panhandle, Wyoming, and Canada.

Greetings from Borger, Texas

Four

THE RANGER AND BRECKENRIDGE BOOMS

"OVER THE TOP", RANGER, TEXAS

Ranger is located in Eastland County. In 1912, the Texas & Pacific Coal Company encountered some oil shows while drilling test holes for coal. In 1917, the firm changed its name to the Texas Pacific Coal & Oil Company. The company's second well, the No. 1 J.H. McClesky, was drilled south of Ranger. On October 21, 1917, the well blew in at a rate of 1,700 barrels of oil per day.

Within weeks of the McClesky oil gusher, the population of Ranger increased from less than 1,000 to more than 10,000. Accommodations for workers were practically nonexistent, and food and other necessities were hard to find. Drinking water was shipped from Mineral Wells, 50 miles to the northeast. Many workers traveled to Mineral Wells for an occasional bath.

"The Boom that Won the War" was attributed to the timing of the Ranger oil boom, which provided much-needed oil to the Allied forces in Europe. The Ranger boom peaked in 1919, as men were returning from World War I. This provided a steady workforce for the oil fields. Former US president William H. Taft visited the Ranger oil field in late 1920.

In the background of this postcard, more than a dozen wooden derricks stand out in the town of Ranger. Train cars of the Texas & Pacific Railroad (T&P) are in the foreground. The railroad was invaluable for transporting both oil field equipment and workers. At the peak of the oil boom, as many as 10 trains a day pulled into Ranger with loads of passengers packed tightly, sitting and standing.

The winter of 1918–1919 was extremely wet, resulting in muddy, impassable Ranger streets. Enterprising men ferried people across Main Street through the mud on a horse-drawn sled, charging between 10¢ and 25¢. Author Rex Beach fictionalized the Ranger oil boom in his book *Flowing Gold* (1922), which was later made into a 1940 movie of the same name.

Hagaman Lake (misspelled on this postcard) and the Hagaman oil-tank farm were located northeast of town. The city of Ranger was incorporated in 1919, and M.H. Hagaman was the first mayor. He founded the Hagaman Refining Company. Texas author Boyce House wrote books about Ranger, including *Roaring Ranger: The World's Biggest Boom* (1951).

The C.L. Perkins No. 5 well, aflame in this September 13, 1919, postcard, had been flowing at a healthy output of 4,000 barrels of oil and 10 million cubic feet of gas. Other photographs associated with this oil-well fire show a series of seven large boilers set up to produce steam to extinguish the fire.

The "Brewer gusher on fire" may have been either the Texas & Pacific No. 1 or No. 14 Brewer gusher. The Brewer No. 1 was completed in June 1918 at 2,300 barrels of oil per day, and the No. 14 well was completed in November of the same year at 1,500 barrels of oil per day.

CASING HEAD GASOLINE PLANT, RANGER, TEXAS

Casinghead gas plants use pressure to cool natural gas associated with oil, resulting in a product similar to refined gasoline. As with the oil at Breckenridge, 25 miles to the northwest, much of the Ranger oil production included large amounts of associated gas. Processing this gas, rather than flaring it at the well site, was a sound business decision.

Magnolia Davis
3½ miles N of Duke #1

Desdemona is approximately 15 miles southeast of Ranger. The town's oil production peaked quickly, at over 7.3 million barrels of oil in 1919, just one year after the field's discovery. Wells were drilled in the town; as with other early Texas oil booms, many workers lived in tents.

The discovery well for the Desdemona oil field was the Hog Creek Oil Company No. 1 Joe Duke, completed on September 7, 1918, at a rate of 2,000 barrels of oil per day. Magnolia Petroleum drilled the No. 1 Sam Davis a few miles north of the Duke well. A note on the back of this 1919 postcard reads, "Biggest boom ever witnessed. Now in full blast at Ranger, Texas."

243   OIL FIELD SCENE NEAR BRECKENRIDGE, TEXAS

Breckenridge is located 25 miles northwest of Ranger in Stephens County. Drilling for oil occurred in the area as early as 1911 but without success. In 1916, the Texas Company B-1 Parks well, seven miles southeast of town, tested 75 barrels of oil per day with high rates of gas.

Gulf Production Company drilled and completed the No. 1 Stoker and No. 1 Chaney, on the outskirts of town, in early 1918. This was followed by the Gulf No. 2 Stoker, which tested at 12,000 barrels of oil per day and set off the town's oil boom. Before oil was discovered, Breckenridge's population was approximately 500. By January 1920, the population had tripled to 1,500, and by 1922, exceeded 30,000.

91

Big Fire Feb 24 21 Breckenridge Tex.

Johnson 1000 Barrel Well on Fire
Oct 3th 1920
Breckenridge Tex.

Breckenridge sits over a large oil reservoir, and the city allowed drilling in the town. Owners pooled city blocks, and soon, more than 200 wells were drilled within the city limits. Tents set up in vacant lots housed many of the oil field workers. The *Breckenridge American* newspaper reported on a February 24, 1921, fire. The headlines read, "Flames sweep block 10; loss is $240,000. Hundreds in hotels escape scantily clothed but safe."

The *Breckenridge American* newspaper reported on an October 6, 1920, oil-well fire. The headlines read, "Three men dead, result of open cut-offs-oil well fire. City still menaced; conflagration yet to be abated at Johnson well; night of terror for many. Steel tanks save town."

TEXAS HEADQUARTERS, PHILLIPS PETROLEUM CO., BRECKENRIDGE, TEXAS

After the 1918 discovery of the large gas reserves in the Texas Panhandle, Phillips Petroleum became involved in the growing natural gas industry. By 1925, the company, which specialized in extracting liquids from gas, was the nation's largest producer of natural gas liquids. The address of this Phillips office in Breckenridge is noted as the "corner of Williams & Baylor."

Jacob "Jake" Hamon was the principle owner of the Wichita Falls, Ranger & Fort Worth Railroad (WF, R&FW). A line from the town of Dublin to Breckenridge was completed in 1921, after Haman's death in November 1920. The railroad was often called the "Hamon," and for a short time, there was a town along the railroad line named Jackhamon. His name has been written on the train depot in this postcard.

The ground breaking for the Burch Hotel occurred on February 15, 1927. The 10-story hotel opened for business a year later, on February 14. Walker Street, where the hotel was located, was the main commercial street during the Breckenridge oil boom. Shortly after the hotel's opening, a newly formed Petroleum Club moved to the 10th floor.

Moran is located in Shackelford County, approximately 25 miles southwest of Breckenridge. In 1910, gas was discovered in the area with the completion of the Texas Company No. 1 Cottie well. Pipelines provided Moran gas to several towns in the area. Oil was discovered in the area three years later.

Five

NORTH CENTRAL TEXAS

Corsicana is located 55 miles south of Dallas. In 1894, during drilling for deep artesian water, oil was encountered. It was considered a nuisance to the town. Two businessmen thought otherwise and contacted oilman John Galey, who, with his partner James Guffey, completed a well on October 15, 1895. The well had a daily output of 2.5 barrels of oil. They followed this with a dry hole and three wells, each producing approximately 20 barrels of oil per day. (Edward Lynn Williams collection.)

Navarro County's Corsicana oil field was the state's first commercial oil field and produced most of the state's oil until the 1901 Spindletop discovery. In 1896, the field produced 1,450 barrels of oil. The following year, the field produced approximately 66,000 barrels of oil, and by 1901, the yearly production had reached 836,000 barrels of oil. (Edward Lynn Williams collection.)

As oil production at Corsicana rapidly increased, there was an urgent need for a refinery. The J.S. Cullinan Company built a refinery in 1898. The company reorganized as the Corsicana Refining Company, then as the Navarro Refining Company. Magnolia Petroleum purchased the refinery in 1911. By the mid-1920s, the company operated refineries in Beaumont, Fort Worth, and Corsicana. (Edward Lynn Williams collection.)

On January 8, 1923, the Corsicana Deep Well Company No. 1 J.H. Burke well was completed as the discovery well for the deeper Woodbine sands at Powell. The well tested at 400 barrels of oil per day, but within 30 days, it began producing only saltwater. The well nevertheless set off a drilling boom. (Edward Lynn Williams collection.)

Powell oil field is located in Navarro County, 11 miles southeast of Corsicana. The field partially underlies the shallow production from the Corsicana oil field, which had produced oil for 28 years prior to the discovery of the deeper oil pools at Powell. Oil production in Powell peaked during November 1923 at 356,000 barrels of oil per day. By late 1923, more than half of the oil transported by Texas pipelines came from the field. (Edward Lynn Williams collection.)

Tuckertown is located six miles southeast of Corsicana. From its beginnings in mid-1923, this boomtown grew quickly to a population of more than 6,000 within six months. The town included a movie house, two drugstores, a dance hall, and a shooting gallery. With the end of the Powell oil boom, Tuckertown largely faded away by the mid-1930s. (Edward Lynn Williams collection.)

On May 8, 1923, the J.K. Hughes No. 1 McKie, located just over a mile southeast of the discovery well, came in as an 8,000-barrel-per-day gusher. Within 24 hours, the well erupted into flames during workers' shift change. As a result, 13 men burned to death and 3 others died later at the hospital. (Edward Lynn Williams collection.)

Of the 21 oil wells completed in the Powell field during 1923, seventeen tested at a rate of over 1,000 barrels of oil per day, and two of those tested at over 10,000 barrels per day. All 21 wells were drilled to a depth of approximately 2,900 feet. Humble Oil actively participated in drilling at Powell, with a 97 percent success rate—178 oil wells with only five dry holes. (Edward Lynn Williams collection.)

GUSHER Powell Field CORSICANA.

The town of Mexia is located in Limestone County. In 1912, Blake Smith organized 100 local businessmen and formed the Mexia Oil & Gas Company. The company drilled 10 dry holes before a gas well was completed in 1912. By January 1915, forty gas wells had been completed in the area, supplying gas to several nearby towns.

Great Mexia Oilfield. Golden Lane.

F. Julius Fohs, a geologist, teamed up with the flamboyant Col. A.E. Humphreys. Fohs had been working with the Homaokla Oil Company, which had assembled a large block of acreage and had drilled two dry holes. Humphreys, who acquired the block in a deal with Homaokla, predicted that Mexia would be a 100-million-barrel oil field.

The first oil well was completed in November 1920. The Humphreys No. 1 L.W. Rogers pumped at a rate of 50 barrels of oil per day. During the summer of 1921, the Humphreys Company No. 1 T. Berthelson well set off the Mexia oil boom as a 4,000-barrel-per-day gusher. Early oil gushers included the Wood No. 1 (shown here), completed at 17,000 barrels of oil per day.

In 1921, the Mexia field produced over five million barrels of oil. The following year, the field produced 35 million barrels of oil. Peak daily production was 176,000 barrels on February 12, 1922. In less than 20 years, the field produced over 95 million barrels of oil. The population increased to approximately 20,000 by the end of 1921.

Mexia was the first of the Woodbine sand oil fields along the Mexia fault zone. A fault-trapped oil reservoir was an emerging idea in the Gulf Coast at this time. The productive area ran along the fault for over seven miles, with a width of between one-half and one mile. This became known as the Texas "Golden Lane." A note on the reverse of this postcard reads, "More people here and excitement than I can tell you."

Wortham oil field is located in western Freestone County. As additional fields were discovered along the Mexia fault zone, the Boyd Oil Company leased acreage near Wortham and drilled two wells in late 1924. The second well, the Roy Simmons No. 1, produced at a rate of about 8,000 barrels of oil per day. Within three weeks, more than 300 drilling rigs were in the area, including many within the town itself.

The Wortham field was rapidly developed. The population increased from 1,000 to approximately 30,000 in a little over a year. In the peak year of 1925, the field produced approximately 17 million barrels of oil. In January 1925, there were 158 wells producing in the field. Humble Oil entered the area, as did Houston–based Kirby Petroleum Company. When the short-lived boom subsided, the population in 1929 was only 2,000.

This "hot well" in Marlin, Texas, though resembling an oil derrick, is a hot artesian mineral water well, not an oil well. First discovered in 1893, the waters near Marlin were thought to cure rheumatism, arthritis, and even venereal disease. In the 1930s, the city was billed as the "South's Greatest Health Resort."

A 163   HOT WELL NO. 2
MARLIN TEXAS.

GULF PETROLIUM Co. OIL TANKS
ON FIRE MARLIN TEX
SEP 9 1919

On September 19, 1919, an explosion at the Gulf Refining Company's plant near Marlin resulted in $25,000 in damage. The explosion could be heard for five miles, and the associated fire consumed 15,000 gallons of gasoline, a 10,000-gallon crude oil storage tank, and destroyed several buildings.

ADOLPHUS HOTEL   BAKER HOTEL

PHOTO BY PAUL D. CRAVENS

The 29-story Magnolia Building, at Commerce and Akard Streets in Dallas, was completed in 1922. The double-faced, revolving Pegasus "Flying Red Horse" was added to the building in 1934. When Magnolia Oil became part of Mobil Oil Company in 1959, Pegasus remained as the company logo. Mobil Oil moved out of the building in 1977. In 1997, the building was renovated and became the Magnolia Hotel. A new Pegasus had its unveiling on December 31, 1999.

Magnolia Oil Company built the Magnolia Lounge in 1936 for the Texas Centennial Exposition at the Dallas Fair Park. Visitors could rest in the lounge and watch films. The following year, the five-month-long Greater Texas and Pan American Exposition also included the Magnolia Lounge. The lounge later served as a theater, then the park's visitor center, and now as the offices of the Friends of Fair Park.

MAGNOLIA LOUNGE — TEXAS CENTENNIAL EXPOSITION — DALLAS, TEXAS

MAGNOLIA PETROLEUM COMPANY   6A-H1728

Six

WEST TEXAS

The naming of the Santa Rita No. 1 is attributed to Frank T. Pickrell, one of the founders of the Texon Oil & Land Company. During a trip to New York seeking investors for his West Texas oil venture, potential Catholic investors suggested praying to Saint Rita, the patron saint of the impossible. On May 28, 1923, the well, the discovery well for the Big Lake Field, blew in.

Santa Rita No. 1 Discovery Well, Lake Oil Co., Reagan Co. (Texas) Oil Field

The Big Lake Oil Company, a subsidiary of the Plymouth Oil Company, developed the Big Lake oil field. Texon was the first oil company town in the West Texas Permian Basin. The town included a school, stores, a hospital, theater, park, and golf course. The company sponsored a baseball team, a polo team, and Boy and Girl Scout troops.

Loading Racks, Texon, Texas, Reagan Co.

Oil was transported by rail in tank cars and through pipelines. One of the first pipelines transported oil from the Big Lake field, across the state, to the Humble oil refinery in Baytown, Texas. The first oil pipeline in the field was completed in April 1925.

This oil field view in Winkler County, Texas, dated January 12, 1927, is one of the earliest Jack Nolan oil field photographs. The bulk of Nolan's oil field work is from East Texas in the early 1930s. The Westbrook and Company No. 1 Hendrix, completed on July 16, 1926, was the discovery well for the Hendrix oil field. The well tested at 30 barrels of oil per day; after the well was deepened, the rate increased more than tenfold.

Crane County covered 796 square miles. Before the oil boom, the population was primarily ranchers. In September 1927, with the area's population surging from less than 30 to approximately 4,500, a county government was organized. The town of Crane in 1927 consisted primarily of tents and small cabins.

CRANE TEXAS IN THE HEART OF
THE CRANE COUNTY OIL FIELD

Jack Nolan

THE EXPLOSION
OF 200 QUARTS OF
NITRO-GLYCERINE 3000 FEET
UNDER GROUND GAVE MOTHER EARTH
AN AWFUL STOMACH ACHE SO SHE
HEAVED UP ABOUT A MILLION
BARRELS OF MUD WATER ROCKS
AND OIL
STIDHAM THRASHER WELL
UNIVERSITY 1/
CRANE COUNTY

*Jack Nolan
Odessa Tex*

In 1883, a large parcel of land in Crane County was acquired by the State of Texas and assigned to the University of Texas at Austin. The McElroy Ranch acquired the grazing rights. In 1925, George M. Church and Robert Fields of San Angelo, Texas, formed the Church & Fields Exploration Company. The firm completed the county's first oil well in March 1926 on the ranch.

Known for his colorful captions, Odessa photographer Jack Nolan captured this early Crane County gusher. He described the scene this way: "The explosion of 200 quarts of nitroglycerin 3,000 feet underground gave Mother Earth an awful stomach ache so she heaved up about a million barrels of mud, rocks, and oil."

On October 28, 1926, a partnership of the Transcontinental Oil Company and the Ohio Oil Company's subsidiary, Mid Kansas Oil Company, drilled and completed a wildcat well on the Yates Ranch of Pecos County. The well initially tested at over 3,000 barrels of oil per day. After the well was deepened, the flow increased, and on August 18, 1928, it tested at the impressive rate of 70,824 barrels per day.

An aggressive drilling program took place on the Yates Ranch after the discovery well was completed. By mid-1928, 207 wells had been completed and were producing at a combined rate of 2.5 million barrels of oil a day. The Yates field would eventually produce over 1.4 billion barrels of oil.

Largest Producing Well in the South Iraan, Texas

Within a year of the Yates oil discovery, the Ohio Oil Company had 350 workers in the area, living in four different camps. Iraan was the oil boomtown named after Ira and Ann Yates. In less than four years, the town's population had reached approximately 1,600. In this postcard of one of the company's wellheads, separator tanks are visible in the background. (Susan Davidek Svec collection.)

RED BARN TEX WHERE THE WORLD'S LARGEST OIL WELLS ARE FOUND

Redbarn, Texas, was an oil boomtown located in eastern Pecos County, near the Yates oil field. The town was named for a red barn on the Yates ranch that was converted to a bunkhouse for oil field workers. The town consisted of a post office, hotel, café, and a general store. The town was abandoned in the early 1950s.

This, perhaps Jack Nolan's most famous oil field photograph, bears the caption, "A great Texas gusher fire the most unusual picture ever taken in an oil field snaped [sic] the instant the well burst into flames." Another version of this photograph identifies the well as the "Skelly–Amarada Univ. No. 1 Ector County." The location of this well has also been placed near the town of Penwell in Ector County, and is dated April 27, 1930.

The city of Big Spring in Howard County became a refining center for West Texas crude oil. In the early years of Permian Basin oil production, four refineries operated in Big Spring: Richardson Refinery, Howard County Refinery, Great West Refinery, and the Cosden Refinery.

A GREAT TEXAS GUSHER FIRE THE MOST UNUSUAL PICTURE EVER TAKEN IN AN OIL FIELD SNAPED THE INSTANT THE WELL BURST INTO FLAMES. JACK NOLAN

One of Many Large Oil Refineries, Big Spring, Texas   B3

111

12-Story Petroleum Building, Midland, Texas   B7

Home of Many Oil Companies

Josh Cosden opened the Cosden Refinery in 1929. The French company Total purchased the refinery in 1963, selling it in 2000. The refinery, also known as the Big Spring Refinery, is the only one of the original four refineries still in operation. The current owner is Alon.

Midland's 12-story Petroleum Building on West Texas Avenue in Midland was completed in 1928. The Gothic-style structure, originally known as the Hogan Building, was named for Thomas Stephen Hogan, a local attorney and oil entrepreneur. George W. Bush had an office in the building during some of the years that he worked in Midland.

The Scharbauer Hotel in Midland was a well-known meeting place for oilmen during the early years of the West Texas oil industry. The hotel, a project of businessman and rancher Clarence Scharbauer Sr., was completed in 1928. The idea for the Petroleum Club of Midland is thought to have started over coffee at the hotel in the early 1940s. The hotel was demolished in 1973.

Odessa's Permian Basin Oil Show began in 1940 as the Little International Oil Show, as Tulsa held the International Oil Exposition. The Odessa show commemorated the discovery of the Westbrook oil field. The second Odessa show was held in 1941, but there was no 1942 show due to World War II. The third show was held in 1950 as the Oil Field Worker's Show. In 1953, the show was again renamed the Permian Basin Oil Show.

The cast of *Giant* (1956) included James Dean, Elizabeth Taylor, and Rock Hudson. Giant was nominated for 10 Academy Awards, winning one for "Best Director" (George Stevens). Edna Ferber, who authored the novel on which the movie was based, patterned James Dean's character, Jett Rink, on wildcatter Glenn McCarthy. The movie was filmed near Marfa, Texas. Giant was James Dean's last film; he died before the movie was released.

The largest oil field in the Permian Basin is the Wasson field in Gaines and Yoakum Counties. Wasson covers an area of 62,500 acres and has produced more than two billion barrels of oil. Four other fields or trends in the basin have produced more than one billion barrels each: Yates, Kelly–Snyder, Slaughter, and the Sprayberry trend area.

JAMES DEAN in "Giant"   WARNER BROS.

Fuel for a Million Cars a Day!

Modern Oil Field in West Texas

Seven

EAST TEXAS

The Marshall Gas Company was incorporated in Louisiana on September 21, 1906. Gas was discovered in Louisiana's Caddo oil and gas field in 1908. The following year, the company began distributing natural gas to the city of Marshall, Texas, via Louisiana's first interstate gas pipeline.

"Dad" Joiner's No. 3 Daisy Bradford was the discovery well for the giant East Texas oil field. On October 5, 1930, the well tested at a rate of 6,800 barrels of oil per day and was later completed at 300 barrels of oil per day. As hundreds of people came to see the well, cars backed up for more than seven miles. A local farmer charged 25¢ for parking.

In 1931, H.L. Hunt built a four-inch pipeline from near the Bradford well to the Overton-Henderson branch line of the Missouri-Pacific Railroad, three miles away. During World War II, two large pipelines were laid from East Texas to the Northeastern United States. During the war years, more than 350 million barrels of oil were transported by the 24-inch "Big Inch" and 20-inch "Little Big Inch" pipelines.

THOUSANDS OF CARS OF OIL
ARE BEING SHIPED FROM THE
EAST TEXAS OIL FIELDS 237
JACK NOLAN

Sinclair Oil Company agreed to build a loading rack at the rail connection. On December 20, 1930, thirteen tank cars carrying 10,000 gallons each left Rusk County for Sinclair's Houston refinery. Within a year, thousands of railroad tank cars were transporting oil from the East Texas oil field.

HUMBLE CAMP
FROM THE HILL TOP
137
KILGORE TEX JACK NOLAN PHOTO

Humble Oil Company operated at least five camps in the East Texas oil field to house its workers. Two camps were located near New London (Rusk County), and one each near Wright City (Smith County), Turnertown (Rusk County), and Kilgore (Gregg and Rusk Counties). The camps included offices, a warehouse, and housing. The typical employee house had two bedrooms and a bathroom.

Rigs were often pulled from one drilling location to another by a truck or caterpillar tractor, or, in extremely muddy conditions, by draft mules. Mule-drawn and horse-drawn wagons also commonly transported pipe and road-building materials within the oil fields. Both 24- and 32-mule teams commonly hauled oil field equipment.

Joinerville is seven miles west of Henderson in western Rusk County. It was originally called Cyril and then Miller or Miller Schoolhouse until 1930, when it was named Joinerville in honor of Columbus M. ("Dad") Joiner. A post office was established in 1931. During the boom years, the town had a population of 1,500 and supported 35 businesses. This postcard of "Joiner field" shows at least 15 large wooden oil derricks.

Hanlon–Buchanan, Inc. of Tulsa, Oklahoma, advertised itself as a "pioneer natural gas manufacturer" with origins in the early West Virginia oil fields. Its Gladewater, Texas, gas plant, four miles northeast of town, claimed to be "the largest gasoline plant in the world's greatest oil field."

Originally named Cen-Tex Oil, Premier Oil was founded in the 1930s. The company's home office and oil refinery were located on Premier Road, off US Highway 80, just west of Longview. At various times, Premier also operated refineries in Arp, Fort Worth, Brownsville, and Baird. The Longview refinery, under various ownerships, operated from 1935 to 1992.

With the oil boom in full swing, oil speculators and lease royalty brokers promoted "get rich" deals in and around the East Texas oil field. Nacogdoches County adjoins the oil-prolific Rusk County to the south, but it was southeast of the limits of the East Texas oil field.

The East Texas oil field made fortunes for oilmen such as W.A. Moncrief and H.L. Hunt. The expression written on this September 1931 postcard, "Whoopee! Dad struck oil in East Texas," may have been the sentiments of many young men and women.

At the end of this "canyon" between rows of steel oil derricks is the Hercules Supply Company's Kilgore store. The company, whose general offices were in Fort Worth, advertised "everything for oil wells," with delivery of supplies to the nearby East Texas oil fields.

Although there is a Turnersville in Texas, this photograph of 10 wooden oil derricks was probably taken in Turnertown, approximately 10 miles southwest of Henderson in Rusk County. Turnertown, an East Texas boomtown in the 1930s, reached its highest population, approximately 1,500, during the boom.

On August 15, 1931, Texas governor Ross Sterling ordered the East Texas oil field shut down to stop illegal oil production and to prevent waste. Along with the Texas Rangers, 1,200 Texas National Guard troops, including infantry, cavalry, and a few World War I–vintage aircraft, patrolled the East Texas oil fields. These mounted "petroleum patrolmen" were returning from inspecting 1,600 oil wells under martial law.

In September 1931, the Texas National Guard set up one camp outside Kilgore and two other camps near the towns of Overton and Gladewater. Texas railroad commissioner Ernest "Colonel" Thompson named the Kilgore camp "Proration Hill."

Harry Sinclair established Sinclair Oil & Gas Company in 1916. The firm was an early operator in the East Texas oil field, producing 4.5 million barrels in 1931. Harry Sinclair owned a racehorse stable, hence this postcard's caption, "Not Harry Sinclair's racehorses but cavalrymen inspecting a Sinclair well in East Texas." These Texas National Guardsmen inspected wells to enforce the proration laws.

By January 1, 1933, the field had produced 234 million barrels of oil. A note on the reverse of this postcard gives the field's dimensions as, "two hundred miles in length and about as wide." With continued drilling, the actual field dimensions were established as 42 miles long with an average width of four and one-half miles. The oil field, touching portions of five counties, had an area of approximately 132,000 acres.

A 1919 advertisement for Joe D. Hughes, "Teaming Contractor," listed 304 Beatty Building, Houston, as his address, with teams located at Humble, Goose Creek, and Crosby, Texas. The company, established in 1896, built roads and canals and advertised, "oil field work a specialty." In later years, the company also maintained a facility near the Pierce Junction oil field. Halliburton purchased the company in 1962.

Ward A. ("Tex") Thornton (1891–1949) was a well-known oil-well shooter and oil field firefighter. He established the Tex Thornton Torpedo Company near Amarillo and worked extensively in the oil field of the Texas Panhandle. He later worked throughout Texas, including South Texas and East Texas. (Susan Davidek Svec collection.)

The Sinclair Oil Company's No.1 Cole, located two miles southwest of Gladewater, Texas, erupted into fire when a spark ignited the oil gusher on April 28, 1931. Tulsa, Oklahoma, oil field firefighters M.M. and Harry Kinley were brought in to extinguish the blaze. Firefighters wearing protective asbestos gear used a nitroglycerin blast to blow out the fire, eight days after the ignition. At least nine workers died and several others were injured. (Susan Davidek Svec collection.)

SINCLAIR NO.1 COLE NEAR GLADEWATER. MOST DISASTEROUS FIRE IN TEXAS OIL HISTORY. TAKING 9 LIVES WITH BUT A MOMENTS NOTICE. 166

Bringing in Humble-Elliott No. 1, Cherokee County's First 10,000 Barrel Oil Well, March 21, 1927, Jacksonville, Texas

The Boogy Creek oil field is located in Anderson and Cherokee Counties, approximately 45 miles southwest of Kilgore. After drilling two dry holes, Humble Oil & Refining Company, in partnership with the Rio Bravo Oil Company, drilled and completed the field's discovery well, the No. 1 Elliott and Clark, in March 1927. The oil field is located on the southeast flank of the Boggy Creek salt dome.

BORING FOR OIL, TITUS COUNTY OIL & GAS CO. MT. PLEASANT, TEX,

Mt. Pleasant, the seat of Titus County, is located approximately 60 miles north of Kilgore. Oil was discovered in the county in February 1936. The town of Talco was a short-lived boomtown associated with the oil field of the same name. During the boom years, there were three oil refineries operating in the area.

The giant Rodessa oil field has produced over two trillion cubic feet of gas and 400 million barrels of oil. The oil field extends from Western Louisiana across portions of Cass and Marion Counties of Texas. Oil was discovered on the Texas side of the field on December 24, 1936, with the completion of the R.W. Norton No. 1 Haywood well in Cass County.

A VIEW OF RODESSA OIL FIELD FROM HIGHWAY, ATLANTA, TEXAS

BIBLIOGRAPHY

Agee, Jane Snyder. *Borger*. Charleston, SC: Arcadia Publishing, 2002.

Clark, James A., and Michel T. Halbouty. *Spindletop*. New York: Random House, 1952.

Elder, Jack and Caleb Pirtle III. *The Glory Days*. Austin, TX: Nortex Press, 1986.

Halbouty, Michel T. *Salt Domes. Gulf Region, United States and Mexico*. Houston: Gulf Publishing, 1967.

Larson, Henrietta M., and Kenneth Wiggins Porter. *History of Humble Oil and Refining Company*. New York: Harper and Brother, 1959.

Linsley, Judith Walker, Ellen Walker Rienstra, and Jo Ann Stiles. *Giant Under the Hill. A History of the Spindletop Discovery at Beaumont, Texas, in 1901*. Austin: Texas State Historical Association, 2002.

Olien, Diana Davids and Roger Olien. *Oil in Texas. The Gusher Age 1895–1945*. Austin: The University of Texas Press, 2002.

Spellman, Paul N. *Spindletop Boom Days*. College Station: Texas A&M University Press, 2001.

Spencer, Jeff A. *Oilfield Photographers—Three Who Captured North America Oil Booms. Frank Robbins, Frank Trost, and Jack Nolan*. Oil-Industry History, v. 12, pp. 45–57, 2011.

Rienstra, Ellen Walker and Judith Walker Linsley. *Historic Beaumont*. San Antonio, TX: Historical Publishing Network, 2003.

Rogers, Alfred. *Ranger*. Charleston, SC: Arcadia Publishing, 2010.

Rundell, Walter Jr. *Early Texas Oil: A Photographic History, 1866–1936*. College Station: Texas A&M University Press, 1977.

Warner, C.A. *Texas Oil & Gas Since 1543*. Rockport, TX: Copano Bay Press, 2007.

Wilson, Jane Spraggins and James A. Wilson. *Texon, Legacy of an Oil Town*. Charleston, SC: Arcadia Publishing, 2011.

www.tshaonline.org.

www.victoriamanning.com.

Discover Thousands of Local History Books
Featuring Millions of Vintage Images

Arcadia Publishing, the leading local history publisher in the United States, is committed to making history accessible and meaningful through publishing books that celebrate and preserve the heritage of America's people and places.

Find more books like this at
www.arcadiapublishing.com

`Search for your hometown history, your old stomping grounds, and even your favorite sports team.

Consistent with our mission to preserve history on a local level, this book was printed in South Carolina on American-made paper and manufactured entirely in the United States. Products carrying the accredited Forest Stewardship Council (FSC) label are printed on 100 percent FSC-certified paper.

MADE IN THE USA